Potholes in Glen Arcadia

Artist's Dream in Glen Arcadia

A WALK THROUGH
WATKINS GLEN
Water's Sculpture in Stone

TONY INGRAHAM

OWL GORGE PRODUCTIONS
ITHACA, NEW YORK

This book is dedicated to my wife, Liz, for all of her love, encouragement, support, enthusiasm, patience, and outstanding editorial skills and guidance.

On the Cover: Rainbow Falls

All photographs by the author except where otherwise noted

Copyright © 2008 by Anthony D. Ingraham
All Rights Reserved
First published in the United States by:

Owl Gorge Productions
368 Stone Quarry Road
Ithaca, N.Y. 14850
Phone: 607-275-0344
www.owlgorge.com

ISBN 978-0-615-20121-4
10 9 8 7 6 5 4 3 2 1

Editor: Elizabeth Bauman
Book Design: Linda Mikula
Printed by Finger Lakes Press, Auburn, N.Y.

Late-afternoon sun streams over Cavern Cascade.

Contents

Preface	ix
Introduction with Trail Map	1
1 The Main Entrance and Entrance Amphitheatre	7
2 Glen Alpha	15
3 The Suspension Bridge	23
4 The Narrows	27
5 Glen Cathedral and Central Cascade	31
6 Glen of Pools and Rainbow Falls	39
7 Glen Arcadia	47
8 Mile Point and Glen Facility	51
9 The Indian Trail	55
10 The South Rim	63
11 People and Watkins Glen	69
12 Wildlife of Watkins Glen	77
Afterword	81
Acknowledgments	83

◀ Central Cascade

Preface

This armchair guidebook interprets the natural and cultural history of Watkins Glen State Park in the Finger Lakes region of central New York State.

In these pages, you will explore the glen as if you were hiking on the Gorge Trail one and a half miles from the Main Entrance to the Upper Entrance. Through words and pictures, you'll deepen your understanding and appreciation of this remarkable little canyon as you discover secrets of its rocks, water, plants, animals, and people. You'll take an imaginary walk under mossy cliffs, behind waterfalls, past deep rock pools, through tunnels, and up hundreds of stone steps by rugged walls. You will see the glen at different times of the year, at different times in human history, and at different times in the history of the earth. The story will reveal to you how water created this craggy ravine, from its Ice Age origins to its erosion by Glen Creek. And you'll see how differing recipes of sun, shade, temperature, and moisture produce varied and unusual plant communities.

Your imaginary walk will continue on the rims of the gorge and upstream to the site of an old Civilian Conservation Corps camp. A chapter discusses changes in people's relationship to the glen from before the Revolutionary War, to a mill stream, to a Victorian resort, to the state park. A final section explores the animals that live in the park.

This book is not intended to be read while you are walking the trails, though you may choose to do so. There are excellent trailside exhibits that tell much of the story included here. Rather, this is an armchair or camp chair book to be read before or after the experience (or to be read by those who cannot walk the trails), which complements an actual trip through Watkins Glen.

◀ Flood-polished stone layers in Glen Alpha

Introduction

A "book of nature" is how local journalist and promoter Morvalden Ells described Watkins Glen in the 1860s. He was speaking of the splendid natural wonder from which both the town and the famous racetrack take their names.

A "glen" is a ravine, a narrow valley. The ravine called Watkins Glen is cut into the steep hillside on the west flank of the Seneca Lake valley. It is a break in the earth's skin, where a stream has sliced through hundreds of feet of ancient rock layers. For thousands of years, Glen Creek has roared and whispered through its confines, deepening the rugged throat of rock and shaping ledges, pools, and waterfalls. With cave-like gorges, fern-draped cliffs, and splashing waterfalls, Watkins Glen is a sensory delight.

Water created Watkins Glen—water as a stream that eroded the gorge, water as Ice Age glaciers that bored the Seneca Lake valley and changed the course of Glen Creek, and water in an ancient sea where sand and mud settled on the bottom, eventually to harden and become the very rocks the gorge is cut into. The magic of water and its works are what have brought people to the glen, whether to harness water power for mills in the nineteenth century or to walk behind a waterfall in the twenty-first century.

Watkins Glen first opened as a privately owned scenic resort in 1863 as a result of the vision and efforts of Mr. Ells. His descriptions of the gorge and its waterfalls drew thousands of visitors from America and Europe and placed Watkins Glen alongside Niagara Falls, Saratoga Springs, and the Catskill Mountains as a Victorian tourist destination. In 1906, Watkins Glen became the first state park in the Finger Lakes region and it continues to attract hundreds of thousands of visitors each year.

◀ A flood roars through Glen Alpha. *Photo by William Harvey*

Map courtesy of New York State Parks

Rainbow Falls by Captain James Hope. *Photographed with permission at Watkins Glen Public Library*

Travel writer Tip Roseberry wrote in 1982, "A tour through Watkins Glen is a visit to an art gallery of nature, each picture to be savored individually before moving on to the next." In that spirit, let's consider one section of the gorge at a time, starting at the mouth of the glen where it opens to the Seneca valley

In this view of Watkins Glen from Skyline Drive on the east side of the valley, Glen Creek begins on Sugar Hill in the upper right. The stream flows east to the brim of the Seneca Lake valley where it has eroded its gorge called Watkins Glen, which ends abruptly in the village (left of center). ▶

I The Main Entrance and Entrance Amphitheatre

Where Two Worlds Collide

You begin this imaginary hike in Watkins Glen at the Main Entrance down in the village. Trucks roar by on Route 14 at the very mouth of the gorge. Lights blink at the souvenir shop across the street. This is where you make your transition from the busy, noisy world of the twenty-first century to a quiet natural world where time does not seem to matter. From here on, nature takes its own time and follows its own rhythms. What you will find is the result of seemingly endless or beginning-less time, time unimaginably long before humans walked here—or anywhere.

Ice Age Glaciers Set the Stage

The transition between the bustling world of the town and the serene and beautiful experience that lies ahead on the trail is abrupt. It reflects the dramatic intersection of a tortuous little stream valley and a large, ancient ice valley. Glaciers set the stage for the water of Glen Creek to do its work of cutting Watkins Glen.

All of the Finger Lakes are the result of the passage of enormous ice sheets over the region during the Ice Age beginning two million years ago. Glaciers covered New York State in cycles that lasted between 40,000 and 100,000 years. Each glacier melted away and was followed by a warmer "interglacial" period, like the one we are in now.

When glaciers first invaded the region from Canada, they encountered an ancient pattern of small rivers that ran north or south. The advancing ice over-ran the region. But much of the ice was funneled into the river valleys, slowly excavating their courses into deep, steep-sided troughs. The Finger

◀ Entrance Cascade plunges below Sentry Bridge at the head of the Entrance Amphitheatre.

Advancing and melting glaciers from the Seneca valley excavated an ancient river valley and left behind Seneca Lake. Mastodons graze in this artist's conception of the Ice Age at nearby Cayuga Lake. The melting glacier lies at the far end of the lake. *Painting by William Dilger, courtesy of the Museum of the Earth in Ithaca, N.Y.*

Lakes occupy eleven of those troughs. Glaciers dug out the long groove of the Seneca Lake valley in one of the largest ancient river valleys, greatly deepening it and leaving very steep flanks that often form cliffs.

The Play Begins for Glen Creek

After the most recent glacier melted from the lake valley more than 12,000 years ago, Glen Creek established a seven-mile route descending eastward from Sugar Hill, draining runoff from rain and melting snows. The slope and elevation of the hill are similar to what they were before the Ice Age. But the glaciers abruptly sheared off the bottom of the hill near the lake level, where the hillside descends steeply, forming cliffs in some places.

Since the melting of the most recent glacier, Glen Creek has eroded Watkins Glen in the hillside, depositing eroded rock and soil in the lake. Copyright© 2002 Frances Fawcett

The little valley of Glen Creek descends to where it finally drops to the lake valley. It is said to be a "hanging valley," suspended above the deep trough the glaciers dug that now holds the lake. The creek plunges over the brim of the intersection between its hanging valley and the lake trough, forming waterfalls. Over thousands of years, the waterfalls have cut back into the sedimentary rocks of the hillside, gradually eroding the gorge now called Watkins Glen.

The town itself is built on the gorge's disgorgements over thousands of years. Originally the mouth of the gorge fronted directly on Seneca Lake, which extended several miles south of its present southern shore. As the stream eroded the gorge, it dumped rock, sand, and mud into the lake at the mouth of the gorge, eventually creating dry land on the west side of the valley, an ideal place to build the town.

Into the Glen

The Main Entrance to the park is in the last section of gorge for Glen Creek, as it emerges after its trip through waterfalls, pools, and twisting chutes in the gorge. The creek's rush and song will accompany you throughout your walk. Here the stream heads quietly out of the glen, as you will when you return from your walk.

This section of gorge was called the Entrance Amphitheatre by the Victorian operators of the glen because high cliffs enclose you on three sides. At the far end of the Entrance Amphitheatre the towering rock walls suddenly seem to merge, appearing to allow no further passage. A hidden portal reveals Glen Creek where it emerges from its rugged route. Entrance Cascade, the first waterfall, plunges sideways beneath the stone masonry of Sentry Bridge. To the right of Entrance Cascade and Sentry Bridge is Entrance Tunnel, your gateway to the rest of the glen.

Entrance Tunnel enters the cliff to the right of Entrance Cascade and Sentry Bridge.

The staircase inside Entrance Tunnel approaches Sentry Bridge.

The Entrance Tunnel is the first of several tunnels in the gorge. The gorge is so narrow and steep that, after the park was created in 1906, the state park excavated tunnels and walkways to get around some of the cliffs in the glen.

After passing through Entrance Tunnel, you emerge on Sentry Bridge, right above the first waterfall in the gorge, Entrance Cascade. From Sentry Bridge, you can see back into the Main Entrance, while Entrance Cascade is falling right below you. The far end of Sentry Bridge provides your first glimpse into the spectacular interior of Watkins Glen.

Cavern Cascade plunges over the Gorge Trail at the head of Cavern Gorge in Glen Alpha. ▶

2 Glen Alpha

Top: Harebells bloom near Sentry Bridge.

Bottom: Touch-me-nots thrive in the cool, moist shade of the south wall of Glen Alpha.

◀ Cavern Cascade is at the head of Glen Alpha.

When Morvalden Ells gave names to various sections of Watkins Glen, he called some of those sections glens themselves—Glen Alpha, Glen Cathedral, Glen of Pools, Glen Arcadia, and Glen Facility. At the end of Sentry Bridge, Glen Alpha opens up to you. You peer up the stream as it runs toward you through a twisting, narrow, smoothed channel of rock, to crash below you as Entrance Cascade. Beyond, high walls of stone enclose a huge, cool cavity in the earth threaded by the stream and waterfalls. Lush ferns, mosses, wildflowers, and small trees soften the dark, gray stone.

From a stone staircase at the end of Sentry Bridge, you can look back and see the great height of the gorge walls—from the bottom of the Entrance Amphitheatre to the tops of the cliffs above. Little bulblet ferns, mosses, and small wildflowers are at shoulder height as you ascend the steps. In early summer, light-blue harebell flowers with their grass-like leaves eke out a living in a rocky niche. The world is humid and green.

Great Cracks Tell a Story

Across the gorge in Glen Alpha is an impressive cliff bisected by enormous vertical fractures. Stone has fallen from slots between these "joints," as they are called. Joints are caused by compression and expansion acting on rock layers and they are found in rocks throughout the world. Quarries often take advantage of natural jointing patterns in rock formations to remove large blocks of stone.

The layered rocks of Watkins Glen and of central New York State were intensely compressed 200 to 300 million

Huge joints cross the gorge in Glen Alpha.

Flat walls like this one in Glen Alpha result when rock falls away from one side of a joint fracture.

years ago, when Africa and North America collided during a time when the world's continents were aggregating into a supercontinent. The collision resulted in the rise of the Appalachian Mountains to the south and east and the Allegheny Plateau in New York and northern Pennsylvania. The huge joints in Glen Alpha and elsewhere in Watkins Glen are testimony to the tremendous forces exerted on the region during that time.

You can see other evidence of joints and thus the mountain-building period that raised these rock layers high above sea level so long ago. Look around you, and you will notice some very flat, vertical cliff surfaces. These occur where rock has fallen away from one side of a joint, exposing the flat surface of the remaining face of the fracture. Follow a flat surface back to where it joins the rest of the gorge wall and you will see a joint. You will pass many more joints during the rest of your walk.

Where Water Does Its Work

In the middle of Glen Alpha, a staircase descends to a little landing lower in the gorge. Here, you are closer to the stream and in the middle of the gorge. A stupendous rocky scene rises around you. Two waterfalls are visible upstream, and the creek follows a twisting, polished path in the other direction toward Entrance Cascade.

The cliffs above are rough and broken, with a tree here and a shrub there on the slope of rocky debris at the bottom. But down along the stream, the steep, rocky flanks of the creek are smooth and winding with very few plants. This is the flood zone, scraped by sand, gravel, and stones in torrents caused by heavy rain or melting snow, one front line of downward erosion, where floods deepen the glen and smooth its rock.

Looking upstream, in the middle distance there is a waterfall that plunges into a two-part pool. It's called Minnehaha Falls, named by the early proprietors of Watkins

Above: Minnehaha Falls and Cavern Cascade in Cavern Gorge behind

Right: The flood zone

Glen, probably by Morvalden Ells. Minnehaha was the Indian maiden courted by Hiawatha in *Song of Hiawatha* by Henry Wadsworth Longfellow. The poet named her after the original Minnehaha Falls near Minneapolis.

On the stone stairs that climb beside Minnehaha Falls, you can see that Minnehaha Pool is heart-shaped. Years ago, an Indian legend was invented and ascribed to this unique formation. It was claimed that Minnehaha was a local Indian maiden who died, perhaps by jumping off the cliff here following the murder of her lover, her broken heart becoming this pool. But the rocks and water suggest another explanation.

As you can imagine, the base of a waterfall is a place of high energy. The falling water pounds and tumbles rocks below it. During high water, rocks are washed down the gorge and become trapped in the pools below waterfalls. The energy of the water rolls stones, gravel, and sand around, and they gradually drill a "pothole" into the shale and siltstone of the streambed. Over time, potholes can become quite deep.

Watkins Glen is known for its dozens of potholes. The shape of Minnehaha's pothole, however, is unique in the glen. Most potholes are more or less round. Perhaps the ledge at the top of the waterfall directed flow over to the right-hand side of the pool long ago, where the falls drilled out the right-hand lobe of the heart. Over time the ledge eroded, and the waterfall shifted to the left, drilling the left-hand lobe to create a double pothole in the shape of a heart.

Walk behind the Waterfall

At the top of the stairs above Minnehaha, you enter Cavern Gorge, so-called because it is narrow and dark, almost like a cavern without a ceiling. At the back is Cavern Cascade, the first of two waterfalls you can actually walk behind. There is a reason in the rocks why you can do this.

On the way toward the waterfall, the rock wall left of the trail is concave or hollowed away from you. The wall on the opposite side of the gorge is hollowed as well, at the same level. If you look more closely, you can notice a thin horizontal layer of crumbly rock in the middle of the hollow. This is shale, which is easily broken apart by the freezing and thawing of groundwater flowing through joints and between rock layers. The rocks above and below this layer of shale are siltstone, which is harder and has fewer cracks into which water can percolate and, consequently, is much less susceptible to frost. The shale layers are the weak zones in the cliff, allowing the elements to erode the cliff at this level more rapidly all around the gorge. It is this hollowing in the wall that permits you to stand behind the waterfall.

Cavern Cascade is at the head of a little section of gorge. Indeed, most sections of the glen have waterfalls at their

An eroded layer of weak shale in the cliff surrounding Cavern Gorge allowed the trail to be built behind Cavern Cascade.

The Spiral Tunnel ascends from behind Cavern Cascade to an overlooking ledge.

upper ends, because waterfalls have cut them in the first place. There once may have been a pothole at the base of Cavern Cascade being drilled by the force of the waterfall swirling stones, gravel, and sand. If so, the downstream rim of the pothole eroded away long ago. Indeed, Cavern Cascade may have been located back at the staircase where Minnehaha Falls is today, and it may have drilled successive potholes back into the hill, leaving narrow Cavern Gorge behind. This is the way most of Watkins Glen has been formed, by the force of water using stones and grit to drill potholes in the bedrock over thousands of years.

Minnehaha Pool, the plunge pool of Minnehaha Falls, is heart-shaped. ▶

3 The Suspension Bridge

Morvalden Ells described the scene ahead on the Gorge Trail in an 1886 guidebook:

After emerging from the dark chasm, we see before us silvery cascades, quiet pools, and moss-garnished walls, overarched by stately forest trees and thick shrubbery, with a broad light flooding the distance; and far above through the emerald foliage, like a web of gossamer, is seen the beautiful Iron Bridge spanning the Glen.

The Iron Bridge was built in the early 1870s; its original ironwork is still in place today. Now called the Suspension Bridge, it connects the trails on the two rims.

Extinct Waterfalls

Immediately below the Suspension Bridge is a large pothole. It's been called the Wishing Well because people toss in coins while making a wish. Though tossing coins may bring good luck to some people, please don't throw them into the pools in the glen; coins contain copper and nickel, which sometimes are toxic in our environment.

The Wishing Well, however, raises a question. Many, if not most, potholes in the glen, particularly large ones like this, have formed at the base of waterfalls where powerful energy swirls rocks and grit. But there is no waterfall here. Thousands of years ago there may have been a sizable

◀ In the 1800s, the Iron Bridge, now called the Suspension Bridge, connected the Swiss Chalet on the North Rim (left) with the Glen Mountain House on the South Rim. The Glen Mountain House could accommodate 300 guests. The kitchen and dining room were located in the Swiss Chalet, and guests would walk across the bridge, which in some years was protected by a canopy, to eat. The hotel and the Swiss Chalet are long gone, but the original ironwork of the bridge remains. *Copy of Currier & Ives print,* Watkins Glen, New York

The Wishing Well below the Suspension Bridge may have been the plunge pool of a long-gone waterfall.

waterfall pouring into this pothole. In the intervening time, Glen Creek would have eroded the entire ledge supporting the waterfall, leaving the Wishing Well as a relic of a cascade long gone. Perhaps Indians admired this pool's waterfall a thousand years ago. There must have been hundreds of waterfalls that are now long gone eroding the rock of Watkins Glen at levels above your head.

Upstream from the Suspension Bridge, Glen Creek is quiet for a stretch. If you were to stop for a moment before climbing through a short tunnel, you would get a special glimpse of Diamond Falls far ahead in a section of the glen called The Narrows. Beyond the tunnel, you might see lovely wild columbine with its red blossoms perched on rock ledges here and elsewhere in the glen, should it be May or early June when it blooms.

Wild columbine prefers sunny ledges.

When the permanent Gorge Trail was built after the state park opened in 1906, it was necessary to cut into some of the rock walls to create the route. Drill marks are still visible along the path.

4 The Narrows

The sides of the gorge are close together here and little direct sunlight can penetrate. In this cooler and shadier environment, there is less evaporation than in more open sections of the gorge. With the stream confined between damp rock walls below, this is one of the most humid places in Watkins Glen.

The Narrows is lush with ferns, mosses, tender wildflowers, and trees that love these conditions. In the old days, it was called Sylvan Gorge. Perhaps most striking are the trees above on the opposite slope. The tall evergreens are eastern hemlocks, which thrive on shady, cool, steep slopes. Mixed in here and there are yellow birch trees, with their brass-like bark and long roots that cling to the unstable footing.

Beneath the hemlocks and birches are low evergreen shrubs that look like young hemlocks, so much so that some people call them ground hemlock. Actually, they are not hemlocks at all, but rather Canada yew. They live best under the shade of other trees and can hang onto steep slopes and even the edges of cliffs. They make little, red, fleshy berries just as do ornamental varieties of yews. Do not eat yew berries; they are poisonous!

Projecting from the cliffs on either side are shrubby maples called mountain maples. They're most common in the glen in narrow, shady, cool, moist sections.

The microclimate in The Narrows somewhat suggests the cool rainforests of the Pacific Northwest. Similar plants grow there, including the western hemlock, the Pacific yew, and the vine maple. There is one big difference, however. It rarely freezes in a rainforest, while the winters here are hard, and the plants in The Narrows must survive amid massive ice formations.

◂ You can glimpse Diamond Falls far ahead in The Narrows.

Abundant vegetation in The Narrows loves shade and moisture.

Above: Though not common outside of places like Watkins Glen, bulblet ferns appear frequently on damp, shady walls along the Gorge Trail.

Right: Canada yew grows in the shade of hemlock trees on the top of the shady south wall of The Narrows.

Natural Quarrying

Near the upstream end of The Narrows, several large joints cross the gorge, creating Diamond Falls. Freezing has quarried out stone from the joints on the opposite wall. Waterfalls often form where joints cross the gorge because they are weak places where the stream can remove rock along the joint more easily than elsewhere. In this case, there are small joints that run parallel to the gorge and at right angles to cross-gorge joints. Water soaks between layers of rock, freezes, and occasionally pops up a square or diamond-shaped slab of stone. Floods wash the loosened slab down the gorge, usually breaking it up. A ledge is formed at the joint crossing the gorge, creating a waterfall.

Diamond Falls pours over ledges created by large joints that cross The Narrows.

5 Glen Cathedral and Central Cascade

Glen Cathedral is what Morvalden Ells called this section in the 1860s. The high cliffs here do inspire a sense of awe and wonder. And their arching, even overhanging, height might remind you of the interior of some grand cathedral.

From Rainforest to Desert

As you emerge into the light from The Narrows into Glen Cathedral, conditions change radically from where you've just been. If it is a sunny day, you are bathed in light, and the temperature can be much warmer than it was below in The Narrows. On the right, a high cliff faces south toward the sun. Instead of hemlocks, ferns, birch, and mountain maple, you find plants that love sunny, dry, barren spots, including wild sunflowers, goldenrod, wild carrot, raspberries, grasses, and wild columbine. Yet directly across the creek in the shade of the north-facing bank, hemlocks and yellow birch continue to thrive in a microclimate radically different from this one. Here it is as if you've gone from the rainforest to the desert.

A short distance ahead, the hemlock-birch forest that was on the opposite bank disappears, replaced by a huge, high cliff with uninterrupted rock layers. Glen Creek is flowing quietly toward you over flat rocks until it pours into a little V-shaped waterfall to begin its descent to The Narrows.

A Rocky Start

The high wall of Glen Cathedral provides one of the best displays to discuss the origins of the rocks in which Glen Creek has sculpted its gorge. It's a remarkable layer cake of stone rising unbroken to the gorge rim. Along the trail you can see rock layers up close, some of them blocky and

◀ The view back into Glen Cathedral from the stairs that climb to Central Cascade is one of the most dramatic in Watkins Glen.

durable, and others thin-layered and crumbly. The tops of some layers are undulating and rippled. The smooth, blocky rock is sandstone or siltstone, and the crumbly rock is shale.

Much of the earth is covered by sedimentary rocks that formed from particles that are generally the accumulated weathered remnants of other rocks. The rocks of Watkins Glen, and indeed most of the surface rock of New York State extending from the Catskill Mountains in the east almost to Lake Erie in the west, formed from layers of sand, silt, lime, and clay laid down on the bottom of an ancient sea. They were subsequently buried by more sediment until the entire mass was compressed into stone by its own weight and glued together by natural cements in the water. The inland sea that once covered this land no longer exists, but it left its accumulated sea beds behind for us to walk on. The nearest modern ocean, the Atlantic, is 200 miles away.

Notice the vertical joints that rise through the layers in the streambed and in the cliff. Like the joints you saw downstream in Glen Alpha, they are records of a great continental collision between North America and Africa that raised our marine sedimentary rocks into mountains and plateaus in Pennsylvania and New York 300 million years ago. Above, there rose more than a mile of younger layered rocks that have worn away since dinosaur times and perhaps before. Below, another mile and a half of sedimentary rock still rests on deep continental basement rocks more than a billion years old.

South-facing cliffs in Glen Cathedral support sun-loving plants, including these woodland sunflowers, that are not found in The Narrows.

Life in the Sea

The trail passes over some layers of rock that have undulations or scalloped depressions. These ripple marks were made by flowing water hundreds of millions of years ago. They are essentially fossil sea bottoms, preserving the surface that existed when they were soft silt and clay. Occasionally, fossils of marine creatures appear in the rocks. Watkins Glen is not particularly rich in fossils, but you can

Ripple marks in sandstone in the trail are preserved ancient sea sediments.

find them from time to time. (Collecting fossils and other natural materials in the state park is not permitted.)

All of the creatures whose fossils are found in this area became extinct long ago, though related animals live in the oceans today. Some of the most common groups of fossils found locally are brachiopods, which look a little like clams but are not; crinoids or sea lilies, which look like plants but are actually related to sea stars; trilobites, which crawled along the sea bottom and had the world's first compound eyes; and several kinds of corals.

Corals are found in warm tropical or subtropical waters; they generally don't live in the Atlantic Ocean as far north as New York State. Yet there are fossil corals in rocks around here. If corals can live only in warm water, then that suggests that the New York sea was warm, perhaps tropical. Geologists believe that the continents have moved around on the globe during the history of the earth. When the rocks of Watkins Glen were marine sediments some 375 million years ago, New York State was actually a little south of the equator, perhaps at the latitude that Peru is today.

One of several coral species found in central New York State, this staghorn coral fossil is from the Skaneateles Lake area.

A Giant Staircase

You might think of the entire glen as a giant staircase of waterfalls, with each waterfall being a step. The biggest such step lies ahead.

Many sections of gorge in Watkins Glen have waterfalls plunging into them at their upstream ends, and Glen Cathedral is one of the most dramatic examples. At the far end of Glen Cathedral, you come upon a magnificent view of Central Cascade. The great walls of Glen Cathedral come together at the falls, and you must climb another staircase to get to the top. You walk through the final short tunnel and step out onto a stone bridge directly over the waterfall.

Looking back from the footbridge as the water thunders below, you can imagine that Central Cascade is leading the erosion of the immense Glen Cathedral, much as Cavern

Near the top of the stairs from Glen Cathedral, you can see the top of Central Cascade as it plunges below Folly Bridge.

Cascade was eroding Cavern Gorge. From Glen Cathedral to the top of Central Cascade, you are immersed in stone; even the footbridge is made of rock.

The little footbridge was originally made of wood. At one point it was known as Folly Bridge because it was thought foolish to have been built there where it was frequently smashed by floods. Even now, floods come roaring out of the Glen of Pools ahead and rip the stone walls from the top of the bridge every few years.

The tunnel near Central Cascade frames a dramatic view of Glen Cathedral. ▶

6 Glen of Pools and Rainbow Falls

This pothole by Folly Bridge has been finely polished by grit in swirling water.

The remarkable beauty sculpted by water in the rock of Watkins Glen continues to unfold in the Glen of Pools and at Rainbow Falls.

The view upstream from Folly Bridge was called Matchless Scene by Morvalden Ells. Directly in front of you is a shallow pothole that is the staging area for the water's leap over Central Cascade. If there was once a waterfall pouring into this pothole, it is gone now. But the smooth, curved sides of this pool give a good sense of just how finely rocks and sand polish the sides of a pothole, whether below a waterfall or in the course of the stream.

Beyond you can see more potholes in the Glen of Pools. Each pool empties into another. The falls on the upstream edge of each pool are so short they hardly deserve to be called waterfalls. But the pools are magnificent with their charming round contours and green depths as they tumble from one into the next. Near each little waterfall is a joint crossing the streambed that may be where the waterfall and pool began to form. The Glen of Pools winds around the bend and under one of the most beautiful waterfalls in Watkins Glen: Rainbow Falls.

Under the Rainbow

On the approach to Rainbow Falls, you can see a ribbon of water streaming down out of the forest on a green slide of rock. The water then leaps over the trail and into Glen Creek, which has just jumped down Triple Cascade. The scene of Rainbow Falls and Triple Cascade is so lovely and unusual that it may be the most photographed spot in Watkins Glen.

◀ The pothole pools of Glen of Pools drop in a succession of short waterfalls. Rainbow Falls is at the back.

A visitor feels the water in Rainbow Falls in this view from the bridge above Triple Cascade.

You have to be there in late afternoon to see the rainbow.

This is the second waterfall that you must walk behind if you are to continue ahead on the Gorge Trail. You are walking along a natural recess in the cliff caused by the more rapid weathering and erosion of a layer of shale. The waterfall is the end of a small tributary stream that passes through the campground on the rim above.

Most people never see the rainbow. It's best seen in the summer in late afternoon; the sun has to be shining and the water must be flowing readily. You need to stand on the trail on the upstream side of the falls while sunlight strikes the falls from over your shoulder. A spectrum arches through the waterfall.

Mark Twain, who lived nearby in Elmira in the 1860s, tried to convey the remarkable beauty of Rainbow Falls:

> *If one desires to be so stirred by a poem of nature wrought in the happily commingled graces of picturesque rocks, glimpsed distances, foliage, color, shifting lights and shadows, and falling water, that the tears almost come into his eyes so potent is the charm exerted, he need not go away from America to enjoy such an experience. The Rainbow Fall in Watkins Glen (N.Y.), on the Erie railway, is an example. It would recede into pitiable insignificance if the callous tourist drew an arithmetic on it; but left to compete for the honors simply on scenic grace and beauty—the grand, the august, and the sublime being barred the contest—it could challenge the Old World and the New to produce its peer.*

Tiny brook lobelia lives on a sunny, wet ledge along the trail.

Shadow Gorge

Beyond the Rainbow Falls bridge, you emerge into Shadow Gorge, which lets in a flood of sunshine for a short distance. On the right-hand or north side, the cliff rises into the sun. Instead of being a hot and dry cliff, springs drip off it continually. This favors a different plant community than you found in Glen Cathedral in an otherwise similar habitat. In late summer, there are showy flowers, including great lobelia, joe-pye-weed, and wild sunflowers. The ledge along the trail is wet and sunny, and there are tiny brook lobelia.

Because the gorge trends west and east, and the sun is always in the southern half of the sky, Shadow Gorge is half in sun and half in shadow on sunny days. Consequently, the plant communities on either side of the stream are very different from each other. Little can survive on the ledges by the water, as this is the flood zone.

    The opposite bank is in shade most of the time. It too is moist, but the shade favors a lush growth of bulblet ferns. It would be too sunny on the north side of the gorge for these ferns to survive very well.

    At the top of the cliff directly above, hemlocks hang on the edge, mixed among oak trees that like the dryness up there. Downstream and above Rainbow Falls are white pine and red pine trees way up on the South Rim. Pines need lots of sun, so there are few of them in the gorge.

Rainbow Falls becomes enormous icicles in winter. You are not permitted on the Gorge Trail in winter. *Photo by William Harvey* ▶

7 Glen Arcadia

Pluto Falls in Glen Arcadia in the 1800s

◀ Looking into Glen Arcadia from Shadow Gorge: this first section was known as Mystic Gorge, the Narrow Pass, and Spiral Gorge.

The section ahead is the darkest of the glen, perhaps best described by its various names. Shadow Gorge ends abruptly where the walls come together. The corner cliff on the left is decked with hemlocks and was called Pillar of Beauty in the old days. Frowning Cliff rises ominously on the right, leading into dark, narrow, and wet Glen Arcadia. The view from here of its hour-glass pools was dubbed the Artist's Dream by Ells, "where all the beauties of the other glens, silver cascades and crystal pools, light and shadow, sharp angles and graceful curves, foliage, sky and rock, mingle and produce a picture that more resembles an ecstatic dream than anything that can elsewhere be found."

Ells called this first half of Glen Arcadia the Mystic Gorge, the Narrow Pass, and the Spiral Gorge to describe this winding, sculptured passage.

Pluto Falls, "on which the rays of the sun never shine," said Ells, twists through rock halfway along Glen Arcadia. It was named after the Roman god of the underworld, a place of somber, mysterious, and foreboding caverns.

Waterfalls Drill Potholes

The original rock that once filled Glen Arcadia was probably mined out by waterfalls drilling potholes over thousands of years. Large pools suggest that big falls pounded into them long ago, eventually eroding their supporting ledges. Former rims of rock separating potholes have long since broken through, joining pool to pool, like the segments of a worm.

This is, indeed, a barren underworld. The rims of Glen Arcadia nearly seem to close together, permitting little entry to direct sunlight. Vertical and even overhanging rock

Glen Arcadia appears to be the result of the connecting of a series of deep potholes over time.

walls hold no soil, and floods flush out whatever debris might collect below. With little light and soil, plants are few. Several large joints cross Glen Arcadia, creating large rectangular recesses in the cliffs where rocks have fallen out.

Though light may be in short supply, there is an abundance of water, both down in the stream and dripping on your head from the cliffs above. In summer, it feels like it is always raining. In winter, dripping water creates enormous icicles. With its cool darkness, Glen Arcadia is one of the last places in the glen where ice melts out in the spring.

A staircase lifts you from the end of Glen Arcadia above a narrow throat of stone that obscures roaring water, the Arcadian Fall, as it plunges from beneath the arch of Mile Point Bridge.

The bare rock walls of Glen Arcadia have interesting shapes.

Flat, moss-like plants like these Conocephalum liverworts live on damp, shady walls.

8 Mile Point and Glen Facility

Mile Point Bridge is the transition point to the final third of the Gorge Trail, called Glen Facility, probably because it is mostly level and easy. Trails on each side of the bridge lead to trails on the rims of the gorge. Ahead, there are no more dramatic waterfalls, tunnels, and towering cliffs. Instead, this is a quiet, reflective section of the stream. Go around a bend and you will be alone with the soothing sound of the water and the stillness of the trees.

This last section of the trail is a good place to stroll and look at rock ledges, wildflowers, and ferns along the way. A belted kingfisher might swish down the gorge with its rattling call and light on a branch over the stream. A winter wren may sing its long, tinkling melody in the shady hemlock forest rising to the South Rim. An eastern phoebe could sing its name.

Wildflowers, Ferns, and Mosses

In this section of the glen, the creek almost bisects sun and shade. The trail follows the north side of the stream and gets lots of sun flooding down from above the South Rim. This favors the growth of wildflowers, particularly in late summer and fall when wild asters, wild sunflowers, goldenrods, lobelias, and white snakeroot are blooming. The opposite bank faces north and away from the sun and is covered with shade-loving hemlocks and yellow birches.

In other spots, the cliff beside the trail is constantly dripping with springs, supporting algae and bacteria on the sunlit rock. Yet other places along the trail are both damp and sheltered by overhanging ledges or trees. These are great places to see ferns and mossy ledges. The variety of

◀ The railroad trestle near the end of the Gorge Trail spans Watkins Glen 165 feet above the water.

Some damp, shady ledges are covered with mosses.

White snakeroot blooms in late summer along the trail on the sunnier north side of Glen Facility.

A belted kingfisher watches the stream for a meal to swim into view. *Photo by C. Schlawe of the U.S. Fish and Wildlife Service*

At Mile Point Bridge, you are two-thirds of your way through Watkins Glen.

Hard nodules called concretions are exposed in the sedimentary rock layers along the trail. Iron compounds have leached from some layers staining surfaces below.

The railroad bridge was wrecked in the 1935 flood.

conditions along the trail support correspondingly varied plant communities.

At one point, objects that look like cobbles appear in the side of the gorge. They are called "concretions" and are hard nodules that formed chemically in the sediments long ago. They may contain the mineral dolomite, which is similar to the minerals in limestone and is considerably tougher than the encasing shale.

Soon you round the final bend in the trail. Towering above you is a railroad trestle joining the two gorge rims. The creek snakes between its two tall steel piers.

The original railroad bridge was built in 1877 with a single track. That was replaced with a two-track bridge in 1904. In 1935, a great flood swept away the central pier of the trestle, leaving the tracks hanging until they were cut down. The supporting piers of the trestle are set back from the stream now, making them less vulnerable to flooding.

A mile and a half from the Main Entrance, you reach the finale for the Gorge Trail: Jacob's Ladder, a high stone staircase with 135 steps leading to the Upper Entrance to the park. In the *Bible*, Jacob's Ladder is a stairway to Heaven. The park's version of heaven is a snack bar, restrooms, and, at times, a shuttle bus to the bottom. You also find the beginning of the Indian Trail along the North Rim.

9 The Indian Trail

You can return toward the Main Entrance via the Indian Trail following the North Rim. It was said that arrowheads were found along this path and that Seneca Indians had used it to walk from a settlement farther upstream down to Seneca Lake for fishing.

A Walk in the Forest

The Indian Trail takes you through a quiet forest made up mostly of oak and pine trees, including red oaks, white oaks, black oaks, and chestnut oaks, as well as white pines, a few red pines, and even fewer pitch pines. This rim of the gorge receives plentiful sunlight and consequently is drier and warmer than both the interior of the gorge and the South Rim. On a hot day, the Indian Trail can be a hot walk. But it offers something the South Rim does not—three overlooks into the gorge.

Rainbow Falls Overlook

At the first overlook, you get a look at the top half of Rainbow Falls, while the lower portion overhanging the Gorge Trail is hidden from view.

The little brook that feeds Rainbow Falls comes through the campground on the South Rim. It is an example of a small tributary of Glen Creek. Much farther up the glen, there are other tributaries that join the main stream, all of which form a tree-like network of brooks and springs on the east side of Sugar Hill, together comprising Glen Creek's watershed. Its water quality is very good and it supports a variety of stream life, probably because most of

◂ The Indian Trail takes you through an oak-pine forest on the North Rim.

Top: From the first overlook encountered while going down the Indian Trail you can see the top of Rainbow Falls, where a little brook emerges from the forest and the campground.

Bottom: Point Lookout is perched atop this cliff on the north wall of Glen Alpha.

the watershed is forested, with little agriculture or current human settlement.

Glen Creek, in turn, is part of the Seneca Lake watershed, which itself, like all of the Finger Lakes, is part of the Great Lakes–St. Lawrence River Basin. It takes about twenty-four years for the water in Watkins Glen to find its way to the Atlantic Ocean near Newfoundland.

Central Cascade Overlook

At the second overlook, you can see into the Glen Cathedral, the bridge over Central Cascade, and the Glen of Pools. Tall red pines, white pines, and hemlocks crown the opposite cliff. This rim is dominated by oaks and some pines. Particularly common on this side is chestnut oak, which has rough vertical ridges and deep furrows in its bark and leaves that look a little like those of the chestnut tree. Chestnut oaks can live on the dry, rocky soils of the gorge rim. Chestnut trees themselves were once common here, but most were killed by an imported disease in the early 1900s.

Though the Gorge Trail is closed in the winter due to ice and rockslide hazards, the Indian Trail and the South Rim Trail are usually kept open. This overlook is one of the best places to see huge icicles that form in the gorge.

Point Lookout

Continuing down the Indian Trail, you pass the north end of the Suspension Bridge and proceed downhill to the final overlook on the Indian Trail, called Point Lookout. It offers an awesome view into the first section of the glen above the Main Entrance, Glen Alpha. It is a deep chasm, and you can see people on the trail below. From Point Lookout, Cliff Path cuts back down the side of the glen to connect with the Gorge Trail just up from Spiral Tunnel and Cavern Cascade. But if you retrace your steps a short distance, you will find yourself back at the Suspension Bridge.

From the Central Cascade Overlook, you can see the Glen of Pools, Folly Bridge, and two kinds of forest on opposite sides of the gorge. The sunny right-hand side, along the Indian Trail, is dominated by oaks and other broadleaved trees. The shaded left side has more shade-loving evergreen hemlock trees.

James Hope (1818–1892), *Frowning Cliff* (Watkins Glen) 1873. *Collection Arnot Art Museum, purchased in honor of Mrs. Josef Stein, 1987*

James Hope—Resident Artist

Captain James Hope

In the 1800s at the north end of the Suspension Bridge, there was a Swiss Chalet that replaced an earlier smaller cottage called the Evergreen. Visitors could buy snacks and souvenirs, eat dinner, or rest on a porch. Also nearby was the Hope Gallery. Civil War veteran Captain James Hope was a painter in the manner of the Hudson River School. In 1871, Hope was commissioned to create a painting of Rainbow Falls for $10,000, an enormous sum in those days.

Hope was so taken with Watkins Glen that he left his home in New York City and moved to Watkins Glen by 1872. He established his studio and gallery there and dedicated the last twenty years of his life to capturing the beauty of the glen's scenery on canvas. Morvalden Ells and Hope became friends; Hope may have helped Ells name many of the attractions in the glen.

Later Captain Hope's gallery and gift shop were moved to the Main Entrance. The great flood of 1935 damaged the gallery and destroyed some of his paintings. Some of his remaining works are owned by museums in cities throughout the Northeast.

Above: Nineteenth-century visitors could dine and buy souvenirs at the Swiss Chalet.

Right: *Winter House* by James Hope, 1873, shows the Swiss Chalet and the Suspension Bridge from the artist's studio.
Image courtesy of Questroyal Fine Art, LLC

The Punch Bowl is impounded behind this small dam built in the upper glen in the 1930s where an older, wider gorge section narrows to a more recently eroded rock gorge. ▶

10 The South Rim

The area on the south side of the Suspension Bridge was known as Mountain Park in the 1800s. A three-story structure accommodating 300 guests called the Glen Mountain House was located near the south side of the bridge and slightly to the east, overlooking the rim of the gorge. Visitors to the Glen Mountain House were brought by carriage from steamboats docking at the lake or from railroad stations in the village and the Upper Entrance. The Glen Mountain House was destroyed by fire in 1903.

Though the luxury accommodations of Mountain Park are gone, the state park created some popular amenities just up the slope. Through the oak trees, you can see the South Pavilion, built of stone in 1927. The South Pavilion is the centerpiece of the South Entrance to the park.

There are picnic areas adjacent to the South Pavilion, a parking lot, an Olympic-sized swimming pool, and a large playground. The road to the campground begins at the pavilion.

Into the Woods

The South Rim Trail stays in shady woods and affords no overlooks into the glen. The woods on the glen's north side are sunnier and drier and are dominated by oak trees. Some sections of the forest on the South Rim are mostly hemlock trees with little growing beneath them. Other spots, which may have been cleared and have grown up into forest again, support a lush growth of broadleaved trees, including red maples, black birch, oaks, sugar maple, and some hemlocks. All along the South Rim, occasional red pines and white pines poke above the tops of other trees.

◀ A staircase climbs from Mile Point Bridge along the Gorge Trail to the South Rim Trail.

The Glen Mountain House in Mountain Park was a luxury hotel drawing visitors from America and Europe. An Amusement Hall nearby was opened in 1882, "embracing a billiard parlor, a bowling alley, and a music hall for evening hops and other entertainments." *Courtesy of Finger Lakes State Parks*

The campground is large and forested with more than 300 campsites, most of them nestled among the trees. There are six campground loops—short, one-way, single-lane roads lined by campsites. The loops are named after the Six Nations of the Iroquois Confederacy, which span across upstate New York. They are the Cayuga, Mohawk, Onondaga, Seneca, Oneida, and Tuscarora.

The Punch Bowl

Continuing west on the South Rim Trail, you will reach the western end of the great railroad trestle over the gorge that marks the end of the Gorge Trail on the other side of the glen. You continue another half mile into an old forest. The glen gets narrower with rock walls until you reach a small dam. This is Punch Bowl Lake.

Campsites are nestled in the forest on the South Rim.

Punch Bowl is in a wide, wooded section of the glen, with no rock cliffs visible. Glen Creek has eroded several versions of Watkins Glen during breaks in the Ice Age. Former gorge sections were buried with rock and soil pushed into them by subsequent glacial invasions. The stream has re-excavated some of those ancient, buried stretches and has cut through new bedrock in other parts of its modern route. Where these two types of gorges meet is often an ideal place to put a dam. The dam was built after the 1935 flood, along with two other dams farther upstream. The dams have served to moderate the effects of floods as well as to provide recreational areas.

On the banks rising from either side of the dam, there are dozens of old-growth white pine trees and some old hemlocks. Stands like this are rare. This is a tiny remnant of what much of the forest in the Finger Lakes must have looked like more than 200 years ago, before settlers cut it.

This stone and wood pavilion is by Punch Bowl Lake.

The Finger Lakes Trail follows the South Rim.

White's Hollow

About half a mile west of the Punch Bowl, a park road connects the roads paralleling the north and south boundaries of the park. This section of Watkins Glen is known as White's Hollow and includes Hidden Valley, a former Civilian Conservation Corps camp that was converted to a 4-H camp. The name Hidden Valley refers to a narrow, secluded section of gorge at the upstream end of White's Hollow, just above the 4-H camp. White's Hollow is a wide, gentle section of Glen Creek's valley. Several farm and mill families lived there in the 1800s, including Melancthon White, who operated a sawmill in 1865.

Following the route of the South Rim Trail is the Finger Lakes Trail, which continues for several more miles in the state park, past Glen Creek Lake, and finally out of the park and up and over Sugar Hill. It is possible to walk on the Finger Lakes Trail from the Catskill Mountains in the east to Allegany State Park in southwestern New York State. This section is also part of the North Country National Scenic Trail, which goes all the way to North Dakota.

Above: Punch Bowl is a quiet place. On the banks on either side of the dam are old-growth white pine trees.

Left: White pines thrive in the sun above shade-loving hemlock trees.

11 People and Watkins Glen

Original Inhabitants

Some local people say that the Seneca people have considered Watkins Glen a sacred place since before the coming of Europeans. It was claimed in years past that the Seneca lived in a village upstream from the main gorge in White's Hollow. The people of this settlement were said to have walked to Seneca Lake along the path known now as the Indian Trail. But it has not been confirmed that an Indian village ever existed in White's Hollow, though possibly Senecas had a seasonal settlement or camp there.

Whether Senecas ever lived in the glen is uncertain, but a few miles south in the Seneca-Catharine valley was an eighteenth century town called She-O-Qua-Gah, home to prominent Seneca leader Queen Catharine Montour. She-O-Qua-Gah was among forty Iroquois towns destroyed by the Continental Army in 1779. Following the war, the Finger Lakes region became part of New York State.

Big Gully

Early European settlers around Watkins Glen saw the land in practical terms. The forest was timber to be cleared for farming and building. The valley was cropland, pasture, or a place for a town. The lake was a transportation route. A waterfall was a site for a mill.

In 1794, the state sold over 350,000 acres to John Watkins and Royal Flint from New York City, including land that is now the village of Watkins Glen and the state park. John's brother Charles Watkins built a mill farther up in the glen. Their younger brother, Dr. Samuel Watkins, inherited 25,000 acres from them, including the glen. After

◀ Morvalden Ells, who first opened the glen to tourists in 1863. *Courtesy of Schuyler County Historical Society*

Samuel Watkins's grist mill in the Entrance Amphitheatre, before it was torn down in 1869

coming to the area from New York City in 1828, Samuel set about improving the village, which had been named Salubria. Soon he consolidated villages nearby and merged them into a new town he called Jefferson, which, in turn, was renamed Watkins in his honor following his death in 1851.

Local farmers considered the Watkins Glen gorge worthless property and called it Big Gully. Glen Creek was known as Mill Creek. Two other mills were built in the Entrance Amphitheatre, powered by water conducted from above Entrance Cascade. The gorge was a place to grind your grain, not lift your spirits.

The feelings of practical-minded residents of the time were reflected in a verse written by curmudgeon George W. Slawson, who recalled in 1896:

> I played in that glen when I was a lad,
> and the only redeemin' feature it had,
> was the water it furnished for runnin' two mills,
> that were driven by cumbersome overshot wheels
> in the valley below; though I understand's how
> they charge half a dollar for seein' it now.

Freer's Glen

An 1886 guidebook written by Morvalden Ells

Though Samuel Watkins owned Big Gully, it took the vision of another outsider to see a new potential in the sculptured chasm. Morvalden Ells was a newspaperman originally from Connecticut, who moved to Watkins from Elmira in the early 1850s to work on the local weekly newspaper. Ells fell in love with the charms of the glen and realized its potential as an attraction for tourists seeking sublime scenery. He argued that it could take its place among the great attractions at Niagara Falls and Mammoth Cave and bring thousands of wealthy visitors from all over the nation and even from Europe, where a similar movement celebrating natural wonders was taking place.

A local judge, George Freer, married Samuel Watkins's widow and took possession of the gorge upon her subsequent

View at Entrance, Watkins Glen, N. Y.

This is what the Main Entrance to the state park looked like in the early 1900s. *Courtesy of Finger Lakes State Parks*

Portrait of George Freer.
Courtesy of Schuyler County

death. Ells approached Freer and persuaded him to allow Ells to open up the glen to visitors. He improved the wooden mill catwalks in the first sections of the gorge, and on July 3, 1863, Ells opened Freer's Glen. Through the success of his enticing descriptions in newspapers and magazines around the country, he was able to draw between 8,000 and 10,000 visitors to the glen during that first season.

Ells managed Freer's Glen for seven years, writing its first guidebooks. He built wooden walkways, bridges, and staircases far up into the gorge. The pools, fern-draped cliffs, and frothing waterfalls of Watkins Glen gained renown as far as Europe. By the late 1860s, the glen had been sold to new owners and renamed Watkins Glen.

The State Park

In 1899, New York State created a local body, the Watkins Glen Reservation Commission. The next year, the commission recommended that the state purchase the gorge and grounds of the Victorian resort to create the Watkins Glen Reservation. In 1906, New York State purchased 105 acres at the site for $46,512.

In 1924, the state created the Finger Lakes State Park Commission, which took over management of Watkins Glen State Park. The village of Watkins itself decided to change its name to Watkins Glen to avoid confusion for tourists.

The Tree Army to the Rescue

On July 7, 1935, a terrible flood tore through the gorge, ripping out most trail structures. By fortunate coincidence, the Civilian Conservation Corps (CCC) work camp had just opened. Unemployed young men between eighteen and twenty-five years old had arrived at Camp SP44 as part of President Franklin Roosevelt's "Tree Army" to engage in park improvements.

Though it was a heavy blow to the park, the flood's destruction did offer an opportunity to do things differently. The Finger Lakes State Parks Commission adopted principles for park design that stressed the use of natural materials for harmony between park structures and their natural environment. By 1930, park masons had begun the task of replacing concrete trail structures with stone masonry. In 1936, CCC and Works Progress Administration (WPA) laborers put temporary wooden trail structures in place while they engaged in the more arduous two- to three-year project to replace them with stonework. By 1938, the trail reconstruction was largely complete.

Though it was the worst in memory, the flood of 1935 was not the last to damage Watkins Glen. Many more torrents have roared through the glen since, ripping out

CCC men at work. *Courtesy of Dan Costura*

The Main Entrance was devastated by the 1935 flood. *Courtesy of Montour Falls Memorial Library*

Campers arrive at Hidden Valley 4-H Camp.

walls and steps and sweeping stone parapets from the tops of the little footbridges. Damage from rockslides, freezing, and heavy use has required continuous maintenance of the stonework in the gorge. Much of the work of the CCC has been replaced over the decades. Keeping the trails open and safe for visitors is an unending commitment that is kept by crews of park masons and maintenance staff.

Camp SP44 in White's Hollow closed in 1941 as the nation turned its attention to war. But the camp buildings remained. In 1943, the federal government gave the CCC camp to the state park, which slowly converted it to a group camp for rental. 4-H became the principal tenant in 1946, and it has operated Hidden Valley 4-H Camp there each season since. A large dining hall was built in 1979, additional buildings were constructed, and all but one of the original CCC barracks were replaced by more durable structures.

Today, after more than a century as a state park, Watkins Glen remains one of the most popular scenic destinations in New York State.

A member of the Finger Lakes State Parks regional scaling crew removes winter-loosened shale on the face of a cliff above the Gorge Trail in Glen Alpha. This reduces the likelihood that stones will fall on visitors when the trail is open. "Scaling" is an annual spring maintenance project in the gorge that takes weeks to complete.

Watkins Glen becomes narrow again in Hidden Valley, near the site of the Civilian Conservation Corps work camp in the 1930s and now used by Hidden Valley 4-H Camp.

12 Wildlife of Watkins Glen

White-tailed deer are plentiful in the Finger Lakes region. They thrive in the mix of forest, farm fields, and abandoned farmland surrounding the park. Deer prefer not to venture into the rugged gorge, however, and you are not likely to see one along the Gorge Trail. There is little to eat, the footing is treacherous, and they can't easily escape potential enemies. Nonetheless, deer occasionally do blunder into the gorge, sometimes falling to their deaths.

There are other creatures that call Watkins Glen home.

Life in and near the Water

A few birds nest in niches in the cliffs, including eastern phoebes and the dark-eyed junco. The Louisiana waterthrush serenades spring visitors with clear, bright notes from trees above the creek. Though you are not likely to see the winter wren, you can't miss its long, rapid, melodious, and twittering song in the woods above the gorge, particularly in Glen Facility.

You might see a belted kingfisher perching on a branch or swooping through the glen as it gives its long rattling call. The kingfisher likes to dive into the stream to catch a minnow or a crayfish. And occasionally, a tall, gawky great blue heron may venture into the gorge to stalk along the stream bank to pluck a fish with its long, pointed bill.

Ducks rarely frequent Watkins Glen, at least in the gorge itself. The quick, shallow water, the rocky stream banks, and gorge walls are not hospitable to them. They prefer Glen Creek Lake and Punch Bowl Lake farther upstream, where there is vegetation and quiet water. That's also where you are most likely to run across signs of beavers, who build

◄ A garter snake basks on a ledge by the landing in Glen Alpha. Poisonous snakes are not known in the park. Because the gorge is rugged, there are not many animals to be seen along the trail.

This newspaper clipping from the Associated Press demonstrates the fame that a stranded deer achieved in 1933. It stood on a ledge in Glen Alpha for a week and a half before park employees drove it off the ledge, and it left the gorge unharmed. Seeing a deer was uncommon in those times.

their stick-and-mud lodges in the impoundments. Beavers occasionally attempt to make their own dams along quieter stretches of Glen Creek in the western portions of the park.

In the gorge, the stream is a challenging place to live. There are high, pounding waterfalls and deep pools. Sometimes the water roars in flood, and during dry times it is shallow and sluggish. Most of the fish in the gorge are minnows, including creek chubs and black-nosed dace. Small fish, stream insects, and crayfish are constantly trying not to get washed downstream. Entrance Cascade prevents trout and bass that swim upstream from Seneca Lake from venturing past the Main Entrance Amphitheatre.

Life in the Forest

The forests on the rims of Watkins Glen are rich in wildlife. Song birds, such as the wood thrush, scarlet tanager, robin, black-throated green warbler, red-eyed vireo, and others nest in and among the oaks, birches, pines, hemlocks, and maples. So do great horned owls, screech owls, red-tailed hawks, and the large, red-crested pileated woodpecker. Wild turkeys, red and gray foxes, raccoons, striped skunks, opossums, minks, and other mammals common to central New York State are found in park woodlands. Red and gray squirrels chatter in the trees, and a black-furred variety of the gray squirrel is seen in White's Hollow. Uncommon are bobcats and porcupines. Bears rarely venture into the park. There are garter snakes, milk snakes, and black rat snakes, but the park staff knows of no sightings of poisonous snakes. Northern water snakes might be seen near the creek.

Deer populations have varied over time with human changes to the landscape, and so have other animals. The mountain lion, the gray wolf, and the elk are absent from Watkins Glen due to habitat destruction, predator persecution, and over-hunting. Missing is the extinct passenger pigeon, which once flew over in mile-wide flocks. The wild turkey disappeared from central and western

A great blue heron looks for fish in the creek.

Beavers built this stick and mud lodge on the north bank of Punch Bowl Lake.

At night, you may hear coyotes yipping. *Photo by R.H. Barrett of U.S. Fish and Wildlife Service*

New York State but has returned to healthy populations with reintroduction and regulated hunting. Over-trapping and habitat destruction eliminated the beaver, but beavers from Pennsylvania eventually repopulated the area following protection and trapping regulation. The river otter was also wiped out, but is now trying to regain a foothold since reintroduction.

Raccoon populations increased with human settlement, though their numbers may be lower now due to a rabies epidemic that reached the area in the early 1990s. Since the eradication of the wolf and the regrowth of forest on abandoned farmland, coyotes have occupied New York State, including the Watkins Glen area. Their howling and yipping can sometimes be heard at night in woods near the park.

Generally, wild animals in the park are not dangerous, if you use common sense. Don't feed them and don't harass them. Keep pets away from wildlife. Some animals have learned that they can find food in the campground. If an animal looks sick or is behaving strangely, particularly a raccoon or a fox, it may have rabies. If you see wild animals, leave them alone and enjoy them from a distance.

Afterword

Since the Civil War, people have celebrated Watkins Glen's remarkable beauty, and hundreds of thousands visit the park each year. The glen is a refuge to escape the stress and clatter of modern life for a few hours, to soothe one's spirit with the music of water and the balm of lush, green foliage. It is a place to connect with the earth, with the elements, with the richness of our senses, and with life.

The Seneca people, the original inhabitants of the Watkins Glen area, and other Native Americans have great respect for nature and they feel a responsibility for maintaining good relationships with other living things. As you return to the world of town, perhaps you will carry with you some of the spirit of this place. Perhaps you will love, appreciate, understand, and take care of our beautiful world a little more.

Many children who visit Watkins Glen with their parents return to share the place with their own children years later. May Watkins Glen be as beautiful as it is now when today's children come back with their sons and daughters.

◀ Sentry Bridge

Looking down upon Central Cascade from Folly Bridge

Acknowledgments

I want to thank my wife, Liz Bauman, for her wonderful support and encouragement, her professional editorial review throughout, her help with selection of photographs, and her guidance through the publication process. She connected me with Linda Mikula who applied her outstanding talents to the design, and Gerry Mirabito of Finger Lakes Press in Auburn, N.Y.

This book is derived from a master's thesis I wrote for Empire State College in 2004. Geologists Robert Ross at the Museum of the Earth in Ithaca and Clifford Blizard at SUNY College of Environmental Science and Forestry in Syracuse reviewed my manuscript for accuracy. Karen Edelstein, author, ecologist, and former environmental educator on my staff, reviewed my manuscript and made numerous helpful suggestions. I consulted with park staff, including ranger Fred Wyszkowski, park manager Chris Nielsen, assistant park manager Cliff Lott, and park office manager Kristine Kusevich. Sarah Fiorello at the Finger Lakes State Parks regional office helped me with photographic resources. Adrianna Hirtler, Cornell student and intern on my staff, helped me with analysis of the gorge experience. For tourism information, I consulted with Max Neal of the Schuyler County Chamber of Commerce. Jack Brubaker, owner of adjacent Seneca Lodge and past president of the Schuyler County Bird Club, shared his knowledge about park birdlife. Andrew Saunders at SUNY College of Environmental Science and Forestry reviewed my manuscript for interpretive design and environmental sciences. Elaine Handley at Empire State College provided me with essential guidance throughout the master's thesis phase of this project.

Entering The Narrows ▶

About the Author

For twenty-four years, Tony Ingraham was in charge of environmental education in the Finger Lakes Region of New York State Parks, working from the regional office at Taughannock Falls State Park in Trumansburg, N.Y. He developed interpretive and educational programs and media for the public in most of the Finger Lakes facilities, including Watkins Glen State Park. Ingraham hired, trained, and supervised seasonal guides. He led countless visitors through the glen, including tour groups and school groups, interpreting the natural and cultural history of the gorge. He also developed a slide show about the park for the people staying in the campground and a trail guide leaflet for visitors. Ingraham created the system of outdoor exhibits that are now in place along the trails and at trail entrances and junctions.